THE
TINY
PICTURE BOOK

GEORGE W. HOBBS

[ZHINGOORA BOOKS]

THE TINY PICTURE BOOK.

APPLES so round, and bright, and red—
O, how I love to see;
They look so tempting as they hang
Upon the green old tree.

A naughty boy once tried to steal
From off his neighbor's bough;
But sad to hear, adown he fell,
And is a cripple now.

BOYS oftentimes are rough and rude,
And join in wicked play;
But hoop and top, and bat and ball,
Are better any day.

"Hark! hark! I hear a tinkling bell;
It calleth me to school."
Run, run! my boy, and study well;
Keep strictly every rule.

CAREFUL be of poor old puss,
She catcheth all the mice:
If any rat appears in sight,
She chases in a trice.

And then she comes and sits her down,
And washes all her fur;
How kind and loving doth she look—
How pleasant doth she purr.

DOGS are so faithful, kind, and true,
We ought to treat them well;
My little Johnny had a dog,
Of which I wish to tell.

Now little John was at his play
Beside the river's brink—
Plash! in he fell! Good Rover ran,
And would not let him sink.

EGGS are most useful to mamma;
She says she could not make,
Without the help of new-laid eggs,
Good pudding or nice cake.

I'm sure the hens are very kind
To lay for us some eggs;
O, do not stone or tease them so,
You'll break their little legs.

FROGS! frogs! I hear their merry croak
From river, pond, and stream;
O, now I know that Spring has come,
And all will soon be green.

Who would not sing in sweet spring-time,
The time of song and flowers?
Dear children, youth is your spring-time;
Improve its precious hours.

GIRLS should be gentle, soft, and mild;
Never be rough and rude;
It always makes a happy home,
Where little girls are good.

And they should love sweet Jesus, too;
His blessed laws obey;
At morning's light, at evening's shade,
For his kind blessing pray.

HIVES are the homes of little bees,
And when the day is fair,
In busy haste they sally forth
Into the sunny air,

To gather honey from the flowers,
And bear it to the hive.
Buzz—buzz—work—work—the livelong day;
O, how the busy thrive!

"IBEX! what is an Ibex, pa?"
Said little John, one day;
"A strange and funny animal,
Where do they live, I pray?"

"It is a kind of goat, my son,
Whose horns are wondrous long,
They climb the rough and snowy Alps,
With nimble feet and strong."

JUGS that we use are chiefly made
Of stone or earthen ware;
We find them very useful, and
Must handle them with care.

But jugs are sometimes used by men,
To hold their rum or gin—
These are temptations, children dear;
Pray to be kept from sin.

KEGS, too, so useful in their way,
Are tightly made of wood;
We pack our butter and our lard
In kegs to keep them good.

Their form is homely—but if clean,
They very useful are;
The meanest household article,
Requires the nicest care.

LAMB—pretty, little, quiet lamb,
So gentle and so mild;
O, do not be afraid of me,
I'm but a little child.

O, may I be of that dear flock,
Of which the Saviour told;
Within the pastures of his love,
He keeps his precious fold.

MELONS do in the garden grow,
And very fine are they;
Cool and refreshing to the taste,
Upon a summer's day.

And melons grow upon a vine
That creepeth on the ground;
Amidst the green and silky leaves,
The rich, ripe fruit is found.

NEST! O, a little robin's nest!
Up in the apple tree!
Four little eggs all blue and white,
So close and snug, I see.

"Mother, how could a little bird
So neat a nest have made?"
"'Twas God that taught the little bird
How every straw was laid."

"O, how I hate an ugly owl!"
Cried little Johnny Lee;
This is a very silly hate,
In Johnny's heart to be.

Our God did make the hooting owl,
For purpose good and wise;
O, there is nothing we should hate,
But sin's unholy guise.

PIGS we are apt to treat with scorn,
But this is hardly fair.
For very useful is poor pig.
You surely will declare.

He helps to form our sausages,
And they are very good;
His bristles make our brushes, and
His pork we love for food.

QUAILS fill my mind with holy thoughts;
For when the chosen tribe
Were wandering in the wilderness
Jehovah was their guide.

When hungry, to the Lord they cried;
He sent them quails for food.
God will send us, in hour of need,
Whatever is for good.

ROSES are very fair to see,
And fragrant is their breath;
Their soft perfume doth scent the air
The sweetest after death.

O, let us die in holy peace;
And may our deeds of love
Bear witness of a holy life,
A pledge of rest above.

SWANS float upon the waters blue;
How beautiful the sight!
Their snowy plumage, graceful form,
And neck so arched and light!

Old poets say, the swan doth sing
One song with dying breath;
How sweet the thought—with holy song
To welcome coming death!

TIGERS are handsome, noble beasts,
But O, most fierce are they!
With mighty strength and bloody grasp,
They pounce upon their prey.

So beauty is of little worth,
Without a gentle mind;
Though few are handsome, yet we all
Can gentle be, and kind.

URNS were much used in olden time;
The bodies of the dead
Were burnt to ashes, and the dust
In urns deposited.

And often, on the tombstones now,
We see carved out an urn,
To tell us all we are but dust,
To which we must return.

VINES form a cool, refreshing shade,
And grapes are fine and fair,
Hanging in purple clusters—O,
They look so rich and rare!

Our Saviour saith, "I am a vine,
My branches shall ye be;
I will abide with you in love,
If ye abide in me."

WOLVES are both fierce and cruel beasts,
And feed on little lambs,
If they perchance do stray away
From the kind shepherd's hands.

We are the lambs of Jesus' fold;
O, may we never stray
From our good Shepherd, lest we lose
The straight and narrow way.

XEBECS are ships with three small masts,
And light and fast they sail,
But cannot stand a boisterous storm,
Or weather a rude gale.

This life is like a wide-spread sea;
And, guided by the hand
Of Him who made us, we sail on
To reach a heavenly land.

YACHTS are small pleasure boats, both light
And airy in their form;
They float upon a summer sea,
But anchor in a storm.

Our anchor is the hope of heaven;
When storms of sorrow lower,
Secure and firm, we will not fear,
Even in the darkest hour.

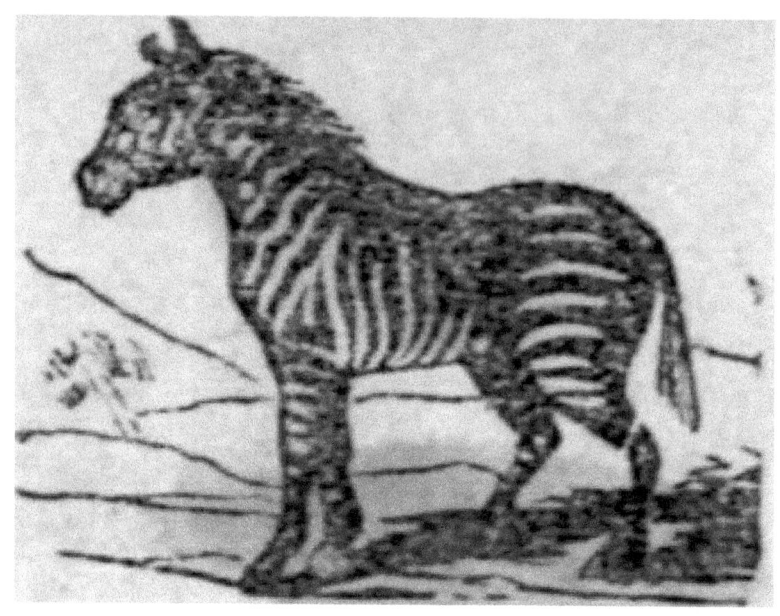

ZEBRAS in form are like our horse,
Though not so tall and slim;
Striped and glossy, smooth and bright,
And beautiful their skin.

They are not docile, like the horse,
They treat man with disdain;
They spurn the rider and his whip,
His bridle, bit and rein.

A, B, C.

"Why must I learn my A, B, C?"
Asked little Kate; "it wearies me.
I wish to put my book away,
I wish to run about and play.
There's kitty in the portico,
O dear! if I could only go;
Indeed, I think it very wrong
To make poor kitty wait so long;
I'll gather pretty flowers for you,
If I may go—do let me, do."

RUN AND PLAY.

Now run away, you little things,
And romp, and jump, and play;
You have been quiet long enough,
So run away, I say.

Fred, you and Lucy roll your hoops;
You on a stick can ride;
And nurse, with baby, run a race,
Or any play beside.

Little boys and girls may romp,
And frisk, and jump, and play;
Book and lessons both are done:
So run away, I say.

End of the book.

www.ingramcontent.com/pod-product-compliance
Lightning Source LLC
Chambersburg PA
CBHW060018300526
45794CB00003B/1211